Old Aberfeldy

with Weem, Fortingall and Glenlyon

by Fiona Grant

Up until the mid-twentieth century travelling folk were a familiar sight in Highland Perthshire. Indigenous Gaelic-speaking Scots, the tinkers, as they were known, would travel in small family groups, pitching their bow-tents on the edge of villages and making their living mending pots and pans, dealing in scrap iron and selling hand-made trinkets. Some found seasonal work on farms and fished the rivers for fresh water pearls. The tinkers would bring news and entertainment to the community. Many were accomplished musicians and, like the man pictured here, could add to their income playing the pipes. The thatched cottage in the background is Clematis Cottage in Weem.

Text © Fiona Grant, 2009.
First published in the United Kingdom, 2009,
reprint 2012
by Stenlake Publishing Ltd.
01290 551122
www.stenlake.co.uk
ISBN 9781840334784

Twin Trees, Kenmore Road, Aberfeldy

Acknowledgements

My warmest thanks go to Henry Steuart Fothringham, Donald Crystal, Ruary Mackenzie Dodds and Mervyn Browne. Thank you as well to James Irvine Robertson; Rosie and Neil Hooper of the James M. MacLaren Society; Carole Wilson; Tom Beels and the folks at Abbeyfield, in particular Jack Kininmonth and Isa Cummings.

Further Reading

The books listed below were used by the author during her research. None of them is available from Stenlake Publishing. Those interested in finding out more are advised to contact their local bookshop or reference library.

Breadalbane Heritage Society and Perth and Kinross Heritage Trust, *Around Aberfeldy*, 2008.

James Fisher, *Memories of an Aberfeldy Childhood*, Impact Communications, 1989.

Duncan Fraser, *Highland Perthshire*, Montrose Standard Press, 1973.

John Gifford, *Perth and Kinross, (The Buildings of Scotland)*, Yale University Press, 2007.

William A. Gillies, *In Famed Breadalbane*, The Munro Press, 1938.

N.D. Mackay, *Aberfeldy Past And Present*, The Town Council of Aberfeldy, 1954.

Hugh MacMillan, *The Highland Tay*, H. Virtue and Company Ltd, 1901.

Perth and Kinross Heritage Trust, *Fortingall Kirk and Village*, 2003.

Jack Rees, *Never an Old Tin Hut*, Aberfeldy Golf Club, 1994.

Alexandra Stewart, *Daughters of the Glen*, Leura Press, 1986.

H.A. Vallance, *The Highland Railway*, David St John Thomas David & Charles, fourth ed., 1985.

These two oak trees, known as the 'Twin Trees', stand on the north verge of the Kenmore road one mile west of Aberfeldy. Local folklore holds that those who cannot pass between the gnarled trunks will forever remain unwed and in times past it would have been a common sight to see locals and visitors squeezing through the two trees. This photograph was taken about 1914 and the tradition was observed until well into the twentieth century. The fact that the two trunks have grown increasingly closer together over the years and the current speed of traffic on that stretch of road possibly account for the custom having died out.

Introduction

Aberfeldy takes its name from the Moness burn that runs through the town before joining the Tay a short distance to the north. 'Aber' means 'mouth of' and 'Pheallaidh', the original name of the Moness burn, is the name of an ancient water spirit that was supposed to inhabit its upper reaches. This region of Highland Perthshire had been inhabited since Neolithic times and remains of prehistoric settlements, burial mounds and stone circles can still be seen in the district. In the Medieval period important religious centres emerged at Weem, Dull, Fortingall and Glenlyon but the area now occupied by Aberfeldy remained in relative obscurity until the eighteenth century.

In 1733, when General Wade built his magnificent five-arched bridge spanning the Tay, Aberfeldy was little more than a scattering of farms on either side of the Moness burn with a population of barely 300 souls. Weem, on the north bank of the river, was much more of a significant settlement having its own inn, school and parish church. Indeed it was at Weem where Wade based himself while supervising the construction of his bridge. Wade had been sent to the Highlands following the first Jacobite rebellion to build a network of military roads that would open up the region and allow government troops to be deployed quickly should the need arise. One of the most important of Wade's roads ran north from Crieff to Dalnacardoch and entered Aberfeldy from the south by way of the Old Crieff Road.

The coming of Wade's road allowed the development of Aberfeldy to shift up a gear. By 1789 the village could boast an inn, a post office, a school, a blacksmith and a shoemaker. These were soon joined by a baker, two wheelwrights, a miller and two woollen manufacturers. Robert Burns visited in 1787 and was so taken with the natural beauty of the nearby wooded Den of Moness that he wrote his famous song 'The Birks of Aberfeldy'.

For centuries, the land in the area had been in the ownership of the Menzies, Stewart and Flemyng families, but towards the end of the eighteenth century much of it fell into the hands of the powerful Breadalbane Campbells of nearby Taymouth Castle. Under their lairdship the three hamlets of Easter Aberfeldy, Wester Aberfeldy and Moness that lay on both sides of the Moness burn officially merged in 1796 to form the single village of Aberfeldy.

In 1802 the visitor Alexander Campbell observed that the village was 'daily increasing in size, with the building of new houses giving it an air of business and even consequence.' Yet the quality of life for the average Aberfeldy citizen remained fairly basic. John Kennedy, whose childhood memories tell of life in Aberfeldy in the early 1800s, describes the houses of his youth as 'little more than hovels'. A cantankerous Robert Southey, who visited the village, wrote in 1819: 'Aberfeldy is a place which might properly be called Aberfilthy, for marvellously foul it is. You enter thro' a beggarly street, and arrive at a dirty inn.'

Peat, gathered from the hills, was the main fuel used for cooking and heating. The villagers grew their own flax, spun their own cloth and made their own clothes. Food would have been a rather monotonous affair with porridge for breakfast and supper and some mutton broth for lunch. Although everyone spoke Gaelic almost all could also speak and understand English. Agriculture remained the main means of employment in the district but many villagers also earned a living as handloom weavers, tailors, shoemakers, carpenters and masons. The Reverend Hugh MacMillan, who was born in Aberfeldy in 1833, described the place of his youth as 'truly a primitive village with streets of thatched cottages covered with moss, and only a few white-washed slated houses, and two or three old-fashioned shops, principally in the Square.'

The Square was the centre of life in Aberfeldy, a playground for the children, a meeting place for young and old, and an important venue for the many fairs and markets held throughout the year. One of the most popular annual events that took place was the Feeing Market. Held in late October, the whole town would turn out in their best attire and farmers from the district would gather to engage workers for the coming year, sealing the contract with a shilling. The Feeing Markets continued until the beginning of the twentieth century and Aberfeldy's regular livestock auction, one of the biggest in the county, carried on in Market Street until the 1980s.

In September 1842 Queen Victoria passed through the town on her way to Taymouth Castle and hundreds of proud Aberfeldy folk lined the streets to cheer her on. By now the present-day layout of the town had properly begun to take shape. Dunkeld Street and the Square had both taken their present form by 1806, followed by Kenmore Street some thirty years later. Textile mills were active on both sides of the burn and in 1856 a gasworks was built.

The first train steamed into Aberfeldy in 1865. Until its demise a hundred years later, the Aberfeldy branch line was of tremendous social and economic importance to the town. Perth was now less than an hour away and Aberfeldy found itself no longer so removed from the outside world. As Jack Rees writes, 'A loaf baked in Glasgow in the early hours of the morning could be on a tea table at the top of Glenlyon on the same day'. The railway heralded the arrival of visitors to the town, many of whom would spend weeks at a time in rented houses and visiting the local beauty spots of Glenlyon and Loch Tay. Sportsmen, too, flocked to the area, which offered spectacular stalking, shooting and fishing opportunities. They would stay for the season in the grand country houses around the district and bring with them a retinue of servants.

Increasing prosperity brought about rapid change and development. Many of the houses, hotels, shops and villas that form the contemporary landscape of Aberfeldy were built in the 35 years prior to 1914. Socially, too, things had gathered pace. Curling, golf, cricket, football, bowling and tennis clubs were all established and active by the turn of the twentieth century and the Aberfeldy Pipe Band was among the best in the land. There was much celebration when the town was upgraded to a Police Burgh in 1887 and a fair bit of rejoicing as well when John Dewar opened his distillery on the eastern outskirts of town in 1896. By 1901 the population topped 1,500 for the first time, a figure not far off today's population of around 2,000.

Between the wars, trainloads of day-trippers continued to pour into Aberfeldy, many travelling onwards to Loch Tay and boarding the steamboats to Killin where they could continue their round trip by rail. With the arrival of the motorcar, tourists began to travel through the district, staying overnight in guest houses and no longer for as long as a week or fortnight.

Today Aberfeldy is a bustling market town and the main service centre for the surrounding district. In 2002, it officially became Scotland's first Fairtrade town. Tourism and agriculture remain an important part of the local economy although the manufacturing industry remains active at the distillery and at the Glenlyon Tweed Mill, and the mining of barytes takes place nearby at the Foss mine.

The Black Watch Memorial was unveiled in 1887 on a site just south west of Wade's bridge at Aberfeldy. It commemorates the raising of the regiment in May 1740, which took place on the north bank of the River Tay a short distance away. Surmounting the monument's stone cairn is the statue of Private Farquhar Shaw dressed in the original uniform of the Black Watch. Shaw was one of the three soldiers executed in the Tower of London following the 1743 mutiny when the regiment, arriving in England and believing that they were to be imminently transported to the West Indies, deserted and marched north to Scotland. The memorial, which was built at a cost of £500, was badly damaged by a lightning strike in 1910 and a lightning conductor has since been installed. The Black Watch was granted the freedom of Aberfeldy in 1970.

1625.

GRANDTULLY CASTLE FROM NORTH WEST.

Grandtully Castle, which dates from around 1400, was originally a small square keep with mural passages and staircases. In 1525 it was transformed into a Z-plan castle and Redcap's tower was added (the tower on the far right of the photograph and named for the goblin that is said to haunt it). Flemish craftsmen, employed by Sir William Stewart in the seventeenth century, added the pepperpot turrets and gave Redcap's tower its distinctive ogee roof. The massive L-shaped addition to the west and north was added in the 1890s. The castle remains largely unchanged since this photograph was taken in the late 1930s although the ivy was removed at the end of the Second World War and the large sycamore in the foreground, planted by Sir William, blew down in a storm in the 1980s.

5

Loch Kennard Lodge was built in the mid-nineteenth century on the southern slopes of Grandtully Hill four miles south east of Aberfeldy. Hugh MacMillan, in his 1901 book *The Highland Tay*, describes 'a lovely little lake called Loch Kennard with an ideal shooting lodge on its shore, surrounded by a grove of pine trees, with beautiful green lawns, sloping down to the waters' edge. . . . The fishing is excellent and the shooting is one of the best in Scotland letting at a high figure.' Indeed the lodge was occupied by a succession of grand sporting tenants including the Comte de Paris and the Maharaja Duleep Singh. The latter made the record books by bagging the greatest number of grouse shot by one man in a single day. The lodge gradually fell into disrepair in the mid-twentieth century and today there is barely any trace of the building left.

CLUNY FORD, ABERFELDY

18335

The house at Boat of Cluny, built by the Stewart Robertsons in the mid-nineteenth century, stands on the north bank of the Tay just a mile east of Aberfeldy. There had been a ferry across the river at this point since the eighteenth century and it wasn't until 1967 that Mrs Jay Cameron, the last ferrywoman, rowed the final paying passenger across this stretch of the Tay. A popular Sunday outing at the beginning of last century had seen Aberfeldy folk walk to Cluny, pay their penny to the ferryman to row them across the river before walking back to town on the opposite bank. In the famously hot summer of 1955, when the river was as low as it had been in living memory, it was actually possible to walk across the Tay at this point.

Aberfeldy from East.

01481 J.Y.

A view of Aberfeldy as it looked at the beginning of the twentieth century. The stone building in the foreground was built in 1895 and served as the town's abattoir for many years. Prior to this each of Aberfeldy's butchers did their own slaughtering and it wasn't unheard of for townspeople to buy a sheep and have it killed in their back garden. According to the 1911 census Aberfeldy's population reached a high of 1,592 and the building boom of the Victorian era with its hotels, churches, and tenements is evident in the photograph. The railway track, now gone, can be seen here entering the town from the east with the Glenlyon hills and the Ben Lawers massif in the distance.

By 1881 Aberfeldy's population had grown to 1,260 and the town was at the beginning of a construction boom, which saw the erection of many new houses, hotels and shops as well as this 1880 tenement building on Breadalbane Terrace. This was Aberfeldy's first large housing development and further tenements were added to the west in 1886. It wasn't long before the Breadalbane Terrace tenements became known locally as 'The Happy Land' owing to the fact that so many of the flats were rented by newly married couples.

PALACE HOTEL, ABERFELDY.   A 1958.

The Palace Hotel was built in 1889 and the handsome building, dressed with red sandstone, was well positioned at the western end of Breadalbane Terrace to catch the eye of visitors arriving in Aberfeldy by road and rail. The arrival of the Highland Railway nearly 25 years earlier had established the town as a favoured Victorian holiday resort and hotels such as the Palace did a thriving trade. Home Street, the top of which can be seen on the left of the picture, was named after a 'Home for the Sick', which opened here in 1879 and was the precursor to the present-day cottage hospital. The famous Aberfeldy Auction Mart, at the bottom of Home Street, was one of the most important livestock markets in Perthshire until it closed in the mid 1980s. The February cattle and sheep sales held there are remembered as being particularly cold.

Aberfeldy Station, 13 June 1936. The branch line connecting Aberfeldy to Ballinluig on the Highland Railway's Inverness to Perth line was first authorized in 1861 but it wasn't until 3 July 1865 that the single-track line opened to passengers. Although just eight and three-quarter miles long, it had been an expensive line to build with 41 bridges, including one each over the Rivers Tay and Tummel. The arrival of the railway consolidated Aberfeldy's position on the tourist map. Holidaymakers travelling to Aberfeldy would be met at the station by horse-drawn carriages and later motor buses, and from there they could journey to Kenmore to board the Loch Tay steamers to Killin. Passengers could then continue their round tour by rail at Killin Junction on the Callander and Oban Railway. The locomotive in the picture is an ex-Caledonian Railway 0-4-4T of the type used on the branch line for 30 years until the coming of the diesel in the early 1960s.

At the time this photograph was taken of Aberfeldy Station in July 1957 there were some five return journeys a day (except Sundays) between Aberfeldy and Ballinluig with halts at Grandtully and Balnaguard. The station buildings in the picture were actually Aberfeldy's third, both the previous station buildings having been destroyed by fires in 1878 and 1929. Within eight years of this photograph being taken the Aberfeldy branch line fell victim to the Beeching cuts and the station closed on the 3 May 1965, just two months short of its centenary. The site of the old railway terminus is now the Moness Terrace car park but parts of the old trackbed still survive and sections can be walked.

Aberfeldy's two tennis courts opened in 1905 and proved to be an immediate success, especially with the young. However, it wasn't until the 1950s that play was allowed on a Sunday and even then only in non-church hours. The Aberfeldy Tennis Club shares its clubhouse, pictured here, with the bowling club. The lovely timber slatted pavilion, with its deeply swept roof extending over a veranda on rustic columns, is a protected building. White-soled shoes and modern sportswear are now the order of play as opposed to the cumbersome-looking dress of the players photographed here in 1909.

The old thatched dry-stone cottage of Tighnalechan stood until the beginning of the twentieth century at the south end of the Old Crieff Road, on a site almost directly opposite present-day Hawthorn Cottage. Tighnalechan once served as an inn and would have been well positioned on Wade's military road from Crieff to Dalnacardoch as it entered Aberfeldy from the south. When the place was demolished a blackened rafter was found bearing the date 1745. The barrow in the foreground was the type for wheeling in the peats.

Dunkeld Street, Aberfeldy.

19352 J.V.

Dunkeld Street, looking west to the Square. Towards the end of the nineteenth century this street saw some big architectural additions including the Station Hotel, the handsome building on right with the octagonal spire, which was built in 1884. On the opposite side of the street is the unmistakeable conical roof of Messrs P. & J. Haggart, the tweed and woollen manufacturers, who moved from cramped accommodation in Bank Street into these fine red sandstone premises in 1899 and are still there today. The gate on the left of the picture is the entrance to what was then the station yard (present-day Appin Place). The bicycle had been introduced to Scotland in the 1860s and by the 1890s had become a craze. The Edwardian lady in the centre of the photograph certainly seems to have mastered the art.

Dunkeld Street at its junction with the Square. The large premises on the right were built for W. & A. Robertson, grocers and ironmongers, in 1898. For nearly half a century 'W. & A.'s', as everyone called it, was one of Highland Perthshire's largest businesses. The site was taken over by the Scottish Co-operative Wholesale Society during the Second World War. The shop on the left, on the corner of Chapel Street, was demolished in 1939 to make way for the Birks Cinema. At the time this photograph was taken in 1911 the shop sold 'fancy goods' and was owned by Mrs Isabella Macleish. In the middle of the photograph, at the eastern end of Dunkeld Street, it is possible to see the signals of the railway and even the steam of a train as it leaves the station.

The 'Factory', built in 1772 by the Flemyngs of Moness, stood for nearly two centuries at the top of Tayside Place on a site now taken up by Dyers Court housing development. The building originally provided both living and working accommodation to lace and muslin makers from Flanders and the factory's bleachfields were where Market Street now is. It was hoped that the Flanders lace-makers would teach their craft to the local population but the project was not a success. By the early 1800s the top floor of the factory house was used as a meeting place and dance hall whilst the ground floor had been converted into private accommodation.

The Aberfeldy Pipe Band was one of the oldest civilian pipe bands in the country and consisted of ten pipers and four drummers. This photograph was taken soon after the band won first prize in the All-Britain Pipe Band Championship at the 1905 Edinburgh Highland Gathering. The band at that time was under the leadership of Pipe-Major Gavin McDougall (centre, front row), whose father Duncan founded the firm MacDougall of Aberfeldy, bagpipe makers to Queen Victoria, King Edward VII and King George V. MacDougall pipes are considered to be some of the finest in the world. The Aberfeldy Pipe Band played until the early 1960s.

The Square, Aberfeldy.

The Square was planned and laid out as a public space in 1806 and soon became the centre of life in Aberfeldy, the place where everything of interest happened and the location for the town's numerous markets and fairs. The street on the left is Bridgend and the Breadalbane Arms Hotel is to its right. Next to the hotel are the Commercial Bank buildings (now the Royal Bank of Scotland), which were built by Sydney Mitchell & Wilson in 1885. Prior to this the bank was based at Auchrannie, a large villa on Taybridge Road. Tucked into the northwest corner of the Square is the Congregational or Independent church, which was built on the site of the old Independent manse in 1877 to take the place of the old church on Chapel Street. The church on the Square was converted to a community centre and tourist office in 2000.

THE SQUARE, ABERFELDY.

Another view of the Square, this time looking to the southwest. On the left of the picture is Struan House, built in 1891, and at the time of the photograph the premises of John Campbell, draper (it is now the Bank of Scotland). The white building with the dormer windows was for many years the property of D. Cameron & Son (established 1839), booksellers and printers – according to an advertisement they stocked a 'large assortment of gift books and popular novels and an unrivalled section of pictorial postcards'. To its right are the premises of John Fernie, saddler (now Munro's outdoor shop), while the large four-storied building on the far right is the Breadalbane Arms Hotel, the main entrance of which was round the corner at Bridgend.

The Old Crieff Road at its junction with the Square, with Struan House on the right and the distinctive striped awnings of Messrs W. & A. Robertson, grocers and ironmongers (now the Co-operative store), on the left. Wade's military road from Crieff to Dalnacardoch entered Aberfeldy by way of the Old Crieff Road, before crossing the Moness burn over a steep-sided hump-backed bridge and continuing over the Tay through Weem, Keltneyburn, Tummel Bridge and Trinafour to Dalnacardoch. Until the beginning of the twentieth century the Old Crieff Road was a stony lane flanked by bush fringed banks and barely wide enough to allow the passage of an ordinary farm cart. The cottage hospital opened at its southern end in 1910 on a site near the old cottage of Tomchulan, the last of Aberfeldy's thatched cottages.

Breadalbane Arms Hotel, Aberfeldy.

A.1961.

Up until the 1850s the Breadalbane Arms Hotel was actually housed in two separate buildings. The eastern part, with its entrance on the Square, was known as the Caledonian Hotel and catered to mainly local traffic while the Breadalbane Hotel, round the corner at Bridgend, took the coach passengers. By the beginning of the twentieth century, Aberfeldy's hotels were much patronised during the holiday season. But it was the 'Breadalbane' that proved the most popular, not least due to the fact that it offered its guests fishing on Loch-na-Craig and the Tay. McKercher's motor garage opened in the hotel's old stables in the early 1930s. In addition to the garage, Alexander McKercher also ran buses, mainly to the steamers on Loch Tay, taxis and road haulage. He was later responsible for setting up the Aberfeldy to Perth bus service. The garage on the Square closed down in the 1960s.

THE SQUARE, ABERFELDY

B.2298

A 1949 view of the Square, with the Birks Cinema now standing on corner of Dunkeld Street. Mrs Cameron's old curiosity shop had been demolished to make way for Aberfeldy's first cinema, which opened in 1939 with Disney's *Snow White and the Seven Dwarfs* less than a month before the outbreak of war. The building introduced an unusual Art Deco element to the Square and after the cinema closed in the late 1980s it served for a time as an amusement arcade. The building is now unoccupied. The Scottish Co-operative Wholesale Society, on the right of the picture, opened for business in the Square in 1942 and it is still there today.

A view of Bank Street, looking towards the Square, c. 1907. It is interesting to see how the east end of Bank Street looked before the McKerchar & MacNaughton buildings were constructed in 1910. On the right of the picture is the front of A. & M. Robertson, a dressmaker's shop run for many years by sisters Annie and Marjory Robertson (it is now an estate agency); to their left are the premises of Thomas Irvine, grocer (now an architect's office). The man in the apron under the awnings on the left is probably Thomas Cameron, the Bank Street butcher at that time. A butcher's shop still occupies this site today.

A later view of Bank Street as it appeared in early 1920s. McKerchar & McNaughton's emporium, which opened in 1910, included a baker's, grocer's, wine merchant's, draper's, dressmaker's, tailor's, boot dealer's, farm supplier's and manure agent's! It remained in business until the mid 1980s and the building is now occupied by Doig & Sons and a supermarket. To its left is McKercher's garage. Originally a blacksmith from Acharn, Alexander McKercher began his Aberfeldy business with this garage on Bank Street and soon acquired the Ford dealership. He later set up a much bigger establishment in the old stables of the Breadalbane Arms Hotel. On the left of the picture, Reid's Hotel, a Crown Temperance Hotel, would later become known as the Crown Hotel. The building is now undergoing conversion into shops and apartments.

BANK STREET, ABERFELDY

18327

Another view of Bank Street, this time looking west, and probably taken on the same day as the previous photograph. For more than 165 years, the bank from which Bank Street takes its name had its premises in the building set back from the street behind the tree on the left of the picture. The Central Bank opened here in 1834. It became a branch of the Bank of Scotland when it absorbed the Central in 1868 and finally closed as a bank when the Bank of Scotland relocated its branch to the Square in 2001. A solicitor's firm and an ironmonger now occupy the building on Bank Street.

Looking north on the Crieff Road, St Andrew's Church is on the left. This was built as a Chapel of Ease in 1884 and it finally became a parish church in its own right in 1897 when it was disjoined from the parishes of Dull and Logierait. The church has recently been sold to developers and is awaiting conversion into flats and the Sunday service now takes place in the former Free church on Taybridge Road (just visible in the centre of the picture.) The Free church was built in the 1840s on land provided by John, the second Marquis of Breadalbane, himself an ardent dissenter. The other building of importance on the Crieff Road, but concealed by trees on the right, is Aberfeldy Town Hall, designed by the Arts and Crafts pioneer James MacLaren in 1889.

CRIEFF ROAD, ABERFELDY LOOKING SOUTH

VELLO SERIES.

Another view of the Crieff Road, this time looking south. The gateposts on the right belong to Balnearn House and much of the stone wall flanking the road remains unchanged today. The building in the middle of the picture, at the top of the road just before it turns to the left, is the old bull shed, for many years the home of the town bull. At one time Aberfeldy had as many as 150 cows, which would spend the summer days grazing in the town's cow parks, including the golf course. Early club rules stated that 'a ball lying within six inches of manure may be lifted and dropped without penalty'.

MONESS HOUSE, ABERFELDY.

202 194 JV.

Moness House, pictured here in 1927, is Aberfeldy's oldest house and was originally the home of the Flemyngs, Barons of Moness, who held land in the district for 300 years. A stone high on the southeast wall of the house bears the inscription 1758 under the initials RSF and AEF. Moness was sold for £9,600 to the Marquis of Breadalbane in 1787. During the Second World War the mansion served as a hostel for evacuees from Glasgow. It is now a hotel and country club and the grounds around the building are home to a number of time-share cottages.

In 1787 Robert Burns visited the Birks of Aberfeldy and, inspired by their beauty, wrote a song of the same name. His description still holds true today: 'The braes ascend like lofty wa's/ The foaming stream deep-roarin' fa's/ O'erhung wi' fragrant spreading shaws/ The birks of Aberfeldie.' Originally known as the Den of Moness, the Birks are designated as a Special Site of Scientific Interest due to the wealth of trees, mosses and ferns that thrive in the damp conditions beside the falls. A wide variety of wildlife including red squirrels, woodpeckers and sparrowhawks can be seen in the area. A collection of exotic trees and shrubs were planted in the lower section of the Birks by local botanist Bobby Masterton in the 1960s.

CURLING AT ABERFELDY.

The Breadalbane Curling Club was founded in 1853 and the pond at Pitilie, pictured here, dates from 1885. According to club records the pond was built at a cost of £55 and a 'Drawing of Prizes' was organized to help raise the funds. Included among the donated prizes were two pigs, a roast of beef and a box of cigars. In mild winters the Pitilie pond would not always oblige and so in 1925 an artificial rink was built in the field on the west side of Taybridge Road. These days members of the Aberfeldy Curling Club, as it is now known, travel to the rink in Perth.

This photograph was taken around 1904 from the top of Bank Street, looking west. On the right is the Black Watch Inn, rebuilt at the end of the nineteenth century and on the left is A. & J. Scrimgeour, a gentleman's tailors for many years and now the premises of Wade's newsagent. The horse and cart are turning right down Taybridge Road and beyond them is Kenmore Street, an impressive regimented layout of mid-nineteenth century houses that had been built on the site of former flax spinners' cottages. Up until the beginning of the twentieth century many of the lanes off Kenmore Street led to byres and the cows would be turned out every morning to be taken by the 'herd boy' to one of Aberfeldy's four cow parks.

These coaches, heading west along the Kenmore Road, were probably taking their passengers on a jaunt to Loch Tay, six miles west of Aberfeldy. The building on the left is the West Toll House, also known as The Armoury, and was built around 1840. It originally served to collect tolls from road users and the bay window would have provided a clear view of traffic in both directions. The decorative barge boarding and diagonal, shafted chimneys are typical of a Breadalbane estate cottage. Later the house was the headquarters of the Aberfeldy 'A' Company of the 5th Volunteer Battalion Royal Highlanders, part of 'The Black Watch', and there was a rifle range to the rear. The houses on the right are late Victorian villas built at the end of the nineteenth century as a result of Aberfeldy's increasing prosperity.

Bolfracks House, Aberfeldy.

F 31373

Two miles west of Aberfeldy, Bolfracks House was owned by the Menzies clan from the early eighteenth century and indeed an old Menzies burial ground can still be seen behind the house. In 1806 Bolfracks was acquired by the fourth Earl of Breadalbane as part of the Taymouth Castle estate and the house became the residence of Breadalbane's factor. The castellated Gothic frontage was added in the late 1830s and between 1890 and 1914 the house was let as a sporting lodge. When the vast estates of Breadalbane were broken up in 1922, Bolfracks was bought by the Hutchinson family and their descendents still live there today.

Golf Club House, Aberfeldy.

61407 J.V.

Aberfeldy's golf course opened to much fanfare in 1895 on land provided for recreational purposes by the Marquis of Breadalbane. Not all the town were enamoured with the new course, which was on the site of one of the town's cow parks and for the next 70 years, until the last cow left, relations between golfers and crofters were often strained. The original clubhouse, pictured here, was erected at a cost of £250 and comprised of a central locker room with ladies' and gentlemen's cloakrooms. The pavilion was improved in 1970 and an extension was added in 1988. The course was extended to the north bank of the Tay in the 1990s with access over a state-of-the-art fibreglass footbridge.

JV 61405

Between 1725 and 1737 General Wade supervised the construction of over 250 miles of roads and 40 bridges in the Highlands, but it was his bridge over the Tay at Aberfeldy that Wade considered to be his finest achievement. Built in 1733 to the design of William Adam (father of the more famous Robert Adam), the bridge was made from locally quarried chlorite schist and built by master masons from the north of England. For many years it was simply known as the Tay Bridge until the railway bridge over the Tay at Dundee took the title. Despite the unfair comment from Robert Southey in his journal of a *Tour in Scotland* (1819) that 'the foundations are very insecure', Wade's bridge has stood the test of time and the bridge still serves as a public highway.

Sir Robert Menzies planted this elegant avenue of Lombardy poplars in 1897, the year of Queen Victoria's Diamond Jubilee. Prior to this the road, which runs north from Wade's Bridge to the village of Weem, was flanked by blackthorn, beech and briar and was known locally as 'The Hedges'. By the 1970s the poplars had become an increasing danger to passing traffic and were felled. The avenue was eventually replanted with native aspen in 1989 under the organization of the Scottish Community Woods Campaign (now Scottish Native Woods). The trees continue to flourish despite the annual flooding that affects this stretch of the road when the River Tay bursts its banks. The photograph was taken from the top of Wade's bridge and the obelisks in the foreground are two of four that decorate the bridge.

Killiechassie stands in unspoilt parkland a mile northeast of Aberfeldy. The mansion house was built in 1865 to replace an older house about 100 yards further east. Killiechassie takes its name from an eighth-century priest, Cassan, who is believed to have established a cell in this area and the corner stone of a chapel can still be seen on a hillside to the east. The private burial ground of the Stewarts of Killiechassie lies by the roadside just beyond the house.

Despite its name, Weem Central Public School was actually located nearly two miles east of the village of Weem on the Strathtay road. The school was founded in 1901 on land provided by Mrs Douglas of Killiechassie. Prior to this children would have attended the old parish school in Weem. Weem Central closed down during the Second World War but the education board retained the building as accommodation for teachers at Breadalbane Academy until the 1960s. It is now a private residence.

30131. Weem.

Weem, just a mile northwest of Aberfeldy, takes its name from the Gaelic 'uamh' (cave) and is named for a cave in the rock above the village that has traditionally been associated with St Cuthbert. The village, a centre of religious and economic importance, predates the town of Aberfeldy by almost 500 years and is mentioned in papers belonging to the Vatican going back to 1275. The white building in the centre of the picture is the historic Weem Hotel. The houses of Tigh Geal and Tigh Craggan are on the left and right respectively. Directly ahead, in the background, is the east gate of Castle Menzies the scene of the Weem Militia Riots of 1797 that took place in protest at the ballot for the conscription of young men into the army.

The Weem Hotel is believed to date back to 1527 and was originally an old drover's inn consisting of just two rooms. When General Wade completed his network of military roads in the Highlands the inn became one of his King's Houses, a hostelry used by soldiers while in a specific area. Indeed Wade himself is said to have been billeted at the two-storey house attached to the right of the hotel when he was building his famous bridge over the Tay a mile to the south. Over the years additions and alterations have resulted in the substantial building pictured here. The pear tree (growing on the left of the hotel's front wall) was planted in 1805 but has since been cut down. The forested slopes of Weem Rock are in the background.

Sixteenth-century Castle Menzies is a fine example of a large Z-plan tower house. The castle had been the seat of the chiefs of the Clan Menzies for over 400 years and witnessed many of the key events in Scotland's turbulent history. Occupied by the Jacobites in 1715 and again in 1746 when Bonnie Prince Charlie stayed for two nights on his way to Culloden, it was later garrisoned by the Duke of Cumberland's troops. The large Victorian west wing, in the foreground of the picture, was built in the style of the old building in 1840. Older eighteenth-century apartments, not visible, were demolished as they were causing serious damp problems. The castle was sold by the Menzies family in 1914 to pay debts. In 1957 the newly reformed Clan Menzies Society bought the castle and in 1972 set about an extensive restoration programme. The castle is open to the public. The ivy has been removed since this photograph was taken in 1882.

The village of Dull, three and a half miles west of Aberfeldy, was the site of an early Christian monastic settlement and ancient seat of learning which is sometimes claimed to have been the origins of St Andrews University. No traces of the monastery survive today but the stone cross in the photograph is one of four ancient sanctuary crosses that separated the ecclesiastical world from the secular. Two of the crosses are now in the Old Kirk of Weem, one is missing, and the one in the picture was moved to this position by 1900, its arm having been damaged by a bolting horse and cart in the 1800s. The old pre-Reformation parish church was extended in the 1840s and was briefly the headquarters of the Knights Templar in the 1990s. It is now privately owned. To the left of the church is the old parish school, which closed in the 1960s.

Towering above a deep gorge on the Keltney burn, fourteenth-century Garth Castle was one of the lairs of Alexander Stewart, the infamous Wolf of Badenoch. The grandson of Robert the Bruce, the Wolf was renowned for his cruelty and rapacity throughout the Highlands. Back at Garth he famously threw his enemies from the castle's battlements into the churning waters of the burn 110 feet below. Rebels used the castle during Glencairn's Rising of 1654 before surrendering to Monck's troops who burnt it. For the next two centuries the castle remained a ruin before being made wind and watertight by Sir Donald Currie at the end of the nineteenth century. This photograph was taken before the castle was fully restored by the Fry family in the 1950s and today it is a private, if somewhat unusual, residence.

86. Garth.

Garth House, a handsome Gothic mansion, seven miles west of Aberfeldy, was built by Sir Archibald Campbell in the late 1830s. It sits on the original site of Drumcharry House, the early eighteenth-century home of the Stewarts who moved here from nearby Garth Castle. The ship owner and Perthshire MP Sir Donald Currie bought the house and the surrounding 6,000-acre sporting estate in 1880. Currie employed the original architect's son, Andrew Heiton Junior, to aggrandize the mansion with fairytale corner turrets, a castellated parapet to the porte cochere as well as internal alterations and even rechristened the place Garth Castle. It has since reverted to its former name of Garth House and after a stint as a youth hostel in the 1950s and 60s is now a private home.

Church & Yew Tree, Fortingall. 428.

The old pre-reformation church at Fortingall was pulled down to make way for this church designed by architects William Dunn and Robert Watson. With its characteristic crow-stepped gables, eighteenth century-style bell cote and Arts and Crafts sundial above the entrance, it was completed in 1902 largely at the expense of Sir Donald Currie. The inside is noted for its splendid oak barrel-vaulted ceiling and contains a seventh-century Celtic hand-bell and fragments of carved Pictish stones. To the left of the church is the famous Fortingall Yew, now believed to be about 5,000 years old and probably the oldest tree in Europe. A wall was erected around the tree in 1785 to protect it from souvenir hunters and local youths who would light Beltane fires at its base.

The picturesque village of Fortingall, eight miles west of Aberfeldy, owes much of its present appearance to Sir Donald Currie who transformed the village at the end of the nineteenth century from a collection of run-down buildings into a model estate village. Currie employed the architect James MacLaren, a pioneer of the Scottish vernacular style and Arts and Crafts movement, to work on Fortingall. After MacLaren's untimely death in 1890 his plans were completed by his colleagues Dunn and Watson who were responsible for the design of the thatched cottages, known as New Cottages, in this photograph. This 1920s view of Fortingall is very little changed today and the houses in the photograph are (from left to right) Fendoch, the Old Post House, New Cottages (today no longer thatched) and MacLaren's Policeman's Cottage.

Fortingal.

The Glenlyon estate was in decline when Sir Donald Currie bought it in 1885 and one of his first priorities was providing decent accommodation for his estate workers in the village of Fortingall. The thatched cottages in this photograph, collectively known as Kirkton Cottages, were built in 1889 by James MacLaren in the Arts and Crafts style. MacLaren's enthusiasm for Devon villages and old tradition had inspired the thatching.

GLENLYON HOUSE, FORTINGALL

Glenlyon House, on the western edge of Fortingall, had been enlarged for John Campbell, Laird of Glenlyon, in the 1720s. Successive generations of Campbells owned the house until Sir Donald Currie acquired it in 1885, adding the house and land to his neighbouring estate of Garth and Drumcharry. Currie had the house remodelled in 1891 almost certainly to the designs of James MacLaren – although the architect had tragically died of TB at the age of 37 the year before. The house was transformed from a fairly plain two-storied laird's house into a grand Victorian shooting lodge with the additions of an attic storey, a west wing and a circular staircase tower with a new front entrance. The crow-stepped gables, Queen Anne windows and battered chimney seen in this photograph are all typical of MacLaren's beloved Arts and Crafts/Scottish Vernacular style.

PASS OF GLENLYON 626

At the entrance to Glenlyon, the mountains crowd in, the river drops away several hundred feet below and just a narrow pass allows the traveller to enter Scotland's longest glen. The winding road that leads from Fortingall into the glen can just be seen on the left of the picture. The buildings in the centre are the house and steadings of Culdaremore and the arched bridge spanning the River Lyon was built by Archibald Ballantyne in 1793. In the field to the left of the bridge lie the archaeological remains of a Neolithic burial chamber and a medieval moated homestead. Drummond Hill, in the background was the site of Scotland's first experiments with forestry when Sir Duncan Campbell planted part of it in the early seventeenth century. It is now leased to the forestry commission and is planted with larch, spruce and Douglas fir.

MacGregor's Leap in Glenlyon is named for Gregor Roy MacGregor who famously leapt across the River Lyon at this point to escape the pursuing Campbells and their bloodhounds. MacGregor, after avenging the death of a fellow clansman in 1565, had found himself relentlessly pursued by Clan Campbell of Glenorchy and although he escaped that day he was later captured whilst visiting his wife and young son at Carnban Castle nearby. Thrown into the dungeons of Balloch (now Taymouth) Castle, he was eventually beheaded in April 1570. Many years after MacGregor's remarkable feat an acrobat tried to emulate the leap but died in the attempt.

8. Chesthill. House, (Perthshire)

Chesthill in Glenlyon is famous for being the home of Robert Campbell, the commander of the government forces at the Massacre of Glencoe. Campbell had moved to his wife's house at Chesthill and joined Argyle's Regiment of Foot after bankruptcy and ruin had forced him to sell his home of Meggernie Castle. It was from Chesthill that Campbell famously set out to Glencoe in 1692 where the order came to him to 'fall upon the rebels, the MacDonalds of Glencoe, and put all to the sword under seventy'. Campbell became the detested scapegoat for the massacre and fled to Flanders where he died in exile four years later.

POST OFFICE, GLENLYON.

The Glenlyon Post Office is at the centre of the small village of Bridge of Balgie, eleven miles up the single-track road from Fortingall. The name above the door in the picture is P. Gorrie, the owner of the store at the turn of the twentieth century. The 1901 census records Peter Gorrie, then 62 years old, as the merchant of the Glenlyon Post Office and sisters Christian and Catherine McNaughton as the post mistress and sewing mistress respectively. Before the motor mail car was introduced to the glen in 1910, the post was delivered by horse-drawn gig, with the post boy making the outward trip on alternate days and returning the following day. The post office, along with a busy tearoom and shop, is still open today. The house on the right is Oakbank Cottage.

The Toll, Glenlyon

At Bridge of Balgie the Glenlyon road continues ahead to Meggernie, Cashlie and eventually Loch Lyon, but a south turn over a stone bridge just before the castle gatehouse leads onto the Lairig road, pictured here. The road runs south over the shoulder of Ben Lawers past Loch-na-Lairig to the A827 Loch Tay road just a few miles east of Killin. The boy in the photograph is standing where there was once a toll. The low building on the left is the old schoolhouse, now known as Riverside Cottage, and the house in the middle of the picture is Kerrowmore Cottage.

THE ENTRANCE TO MEGGERNIE CASTLE, GLEN LYON.

The gatehouse to Meggernie Castle was built by Sir Ernest Wills in 1922. Wills, who had bought the Meggernie Estate in 1920, commissioned a French architect to design a gatehouse in the style of the castle and the result was this striking baronial building. Unfortunately when work on the gatehouse commenced the builders consulted the architect's plans upside down and ended up placing the large picture window looking out over the road rather than the river. The mistake was finally rectified in the 1950s.

MEGGERNIE CASTLE.

Mad Colin Campbell, so named after a blow to the head in his youth left him violent-tempered and erratic, built the original tower of Meggernie Castle around 1585. His great-grandson Robert Campbell, of Glencoe Massacre infamy, added the elegant modern mansion on the right and replaced the tower's thatched roof with slates. Inundated with debt, thanks in no small part to the building works at Meggernie as well as a lifetime of gambling and bad investments, Campbell sold off Glenlyon's immense Caledonian forests in a bid to pay off his more demanding creditors. In 1684, bankrupt and ruined, he was forced to sell the castle and most of its lands and retreat ten miles east to his wife's home of Chesthill. It is said that the castle is haunted by the ghost of a murdered woman who wakes sleeping guests with a burning kiss on the cheek.